NORSE MYTHOLOGY

LOKI

BY KATE CONLEY

Kids Core

An Imprint of Abdo Publishing
abdobooks.com

abdobooks.com

Published by Abdo Publishing, a division of ABDO, PO Box 398166, Minneapolis, Minnesota 55439. Copyright © 2024 by Abdo Consulting Group, Inc. International copyrights reserved in all countries. No part of this book may be reproduced in any form without written permission from the publisher. Kids Core™ is a trademark and logo of Abdo Publishing.

Printed in the United States of America, North Mankato, Minnesota.
052023
092023

**THIS BOOK CONTAINS
RECYCLED MATERIALS**

Cover Photos: Shutterstock Images (background, Loki)
Interior Photos: Katharine Pyle/Granger Historical Picture Archive, 4–5, 28 (top); Shutterstock Images, 7 (Sif, spear), 7 (Odin, Frey, Thor, boar, Mjollnir), 7 (ring), 7 (ship), 14, 28 (bottom); Semiankova Inha/Shutterstock Images, 7 (hair); The Reading Room/Alamy, 8; Pictures From History/Universal Images Group/Getty Images, 10; Ivy Close Images/Alamy, 12–13, 24, 29 (bottom); PHAS/Universal Images Group/Getty Images, 17; Daniel Eskridge/Shutterstock Images, 18; Marvel Studios/Photo 12/Alamy, 20–21; Archivah/Alamy, 23, 29 (top); Werner Forman/Universal Images Group/Getty Images, 26

Editor: Katharine Hale
Series Designer: Katharine Hale

Library of Congress Control Number: 2022949115

Publisher's Cataloging-in-Publication Data

Names: Conley, Kate, author.
Title: Loki / by Kate Conley
Description: Minneapolis, Minnesota: Abdo Publishing Company, 2024 | Series: Norse mythology | Includes online resources and index.
Identifiers: ISBN 9781098291204 (lib. bdg.) | ISBN 9781098277383 (ebook)
Subjects: LCSH: Mythology, Norse--Juvenile literature. | Loki (Norse deity)--Juvenile literature. | Gods--Juvenile literature. | Divinities--Juvenile literature.
Classification: DDC 293.13 dc23

CONTENTS

Loki cut off Sif's hair as a cruel prank.

CHAPTER 1

LOKI THE TRICKSTER

Thor was the strongest god in the land. He was married to a beautiful goddess named Sif. She had long golden hair. One night, the **trickster** god Loki played a **prank**. He cut off Sif's hair while she slept!

Thor was angry. He threatened to break all of Loki's bones. Loki quickly hatched a clever plan. He would travel to the land of the dwarfs. The dwarfs were skilled crafters who could make new hair for Sif.

Loki asked the sons of a dwarf named Ivaldi for help. They were master crafters and agreed to make new hair for Sif. They also gave Loki other gifts for the gods. The gifts impressed Loki. He made a bet with two other dwarf crafters. They were brothers named Brokk and Eitri. Loki bet they could not make gifts as nice as those made by the sons of Ivaldi. If they did, Loki would give them his own head. The brothers got to work.

Gifts for the Gods

From the Sons of Ivaldi

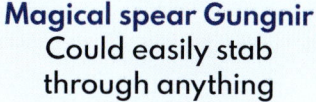

Magical spear Gungnir
Could easily stab through anything

Magical ship *Skidbladnir*
Could fold up small enough to fit in Frey's pocket

Magical golden hair
Would attach to Sif's head just like real hair

Odin

Frey

Sif and Thor

From Brokk and Eitri

Magical ring Draupnir
A gold ring that created more gold rings

Golden boar Gullinbursti
A boar is a wild pig

Magical hammer Mjollnir
An unbreakable hammer that would come back to Thor's hand when thrown

Loki's trickery with the dwarfs resulted in many gifts. The gifts became closely connected to the gods and goddesses who received them.

Loki transformed into a fly to bother Brokk while he worked. Loki hoped Brokk would make a mistake.

When the gifts were done, Brokk and Loki traveled to the land of the gods. They presented the gifts. The gods declared that Brokk and Eitri were the winners.

Brokk demanded Loki's head. Loki said Brokk could have his head but not his neck.

That was impossible! Angry at being tricked, Brokk punished Loki by sewing his mouth shut.

Norse Mythology

Loki, Thor, and Sif are all part of Norse mythology. Norse mythology is a collection of stories about gods and goddesses, giants, dwarfs, and more.

Telling Stories

Norse myths began as stories shared out loud. They were not written down for most of Norse history. The myths changed as different people told the stories. In the 1200s, the first written Norse myths appeared. Because the myths were written down much later, no one knows exactly what the original myths said.

Loki has an endless supply of clever ideas and
plans. He is sometimes good and sometimes bad.

Norse Mythology comes from the religion of early northern Germanic peoples. Most surviving Norse myths come from **Scandinavia**. They are written in the Old Norse language.

Loki is a trickster in the myths. He is also a shape-shifter. He can turn himself into animals. He can also shift from male to female. These traits make Loki hard to trust. But when Loki is near, life is never boring.

Further Evidence

Look at the website below. Does it give any new evidence to support Chapter One?

How Thor Got His Hammer

abdocorelibrary.com/loki

Loki, *right*, is known for playing tricks on others. In one story, he steals treasure from a dwarf named Andvari to pay a debt. Andvari curses the treasure.

CHAPTER 2

LOKI'S LIFE

Loki holds an unusual place in Norse mythology. The Aesir is one group of Norse gods. It includes Odin, Thor, and others. Loki is considered part of this group. But Loki was also part giant. Sometimes he sided with the giants, sometimes with the gods.

The gods were scared of Loki's monstrous children.

The giant Farbauti was Loki's father. Laufey was Loki's mother. Loki had two brothers, Byleist and Helblindi. Odin also treated Loki as a brother.

Loki's wife was a goddess named Sigyn. They had sons named Vali and Narfi. Loki also had three children with a giantess named Angrboda. They were Fenrir, Jormungandr (YOHR-muhn-gan-der), and Hel. A prophecy said these three children would cause trouble for the gods. The gods punished them.

Loki's Monstrous Children

Fenrir was a giant wolf. The gods tied him up with a magical chain. Then they sent him to live in a cave. Jormungandr was a dragon or snake that Odin threw into the sea. He grew to be huge, circling the world. Hel was half woman and half corpse. The gods sent her to rule the underworld.

Clever Loki

Loki is also the mother of Odin's eight-legged horse, Sleipnir (SLAYP-neer). A builder came to the gods. He offered to make a stone wall that would protect them from giants. For payment, the builder wanted to marry the goddess Freya. He also wanted the sun and the moon. Loki and the gods agreed to this deal. But they said the builder must finish the wall in one season, and no one but his horse could help him. The gods did not think the builder would succeed.

The builder and his horse, Svadilfari, started right away. They worked more quickly than the gods expected. The gods were worried about payment. They demanded that Loki fix the problem.

A stone slab from the Viking Age (800 to 1050 CE) shows Sleipnir.

The builder was a giant in disguise. He revealed his
true form when he realized he had been tricked.
The gods called Thor to fight him.

That night, Loki transformed into a **mare**. He lured Svadilfari away from the builder. They ran away together. The builder was angry. He could not finish his work without the horse! He tried to attack the gods. Thor killed the builder. Loki returned months later with a young gray horse named Sleipnir. Loki was Sleipnir's mother, and Svadilfari was his father.

Explore Online

Visit the website below. Does it give any new information about Loki?

The Myth of Loki and the Master Builder

abdocorelibrary.com/loki

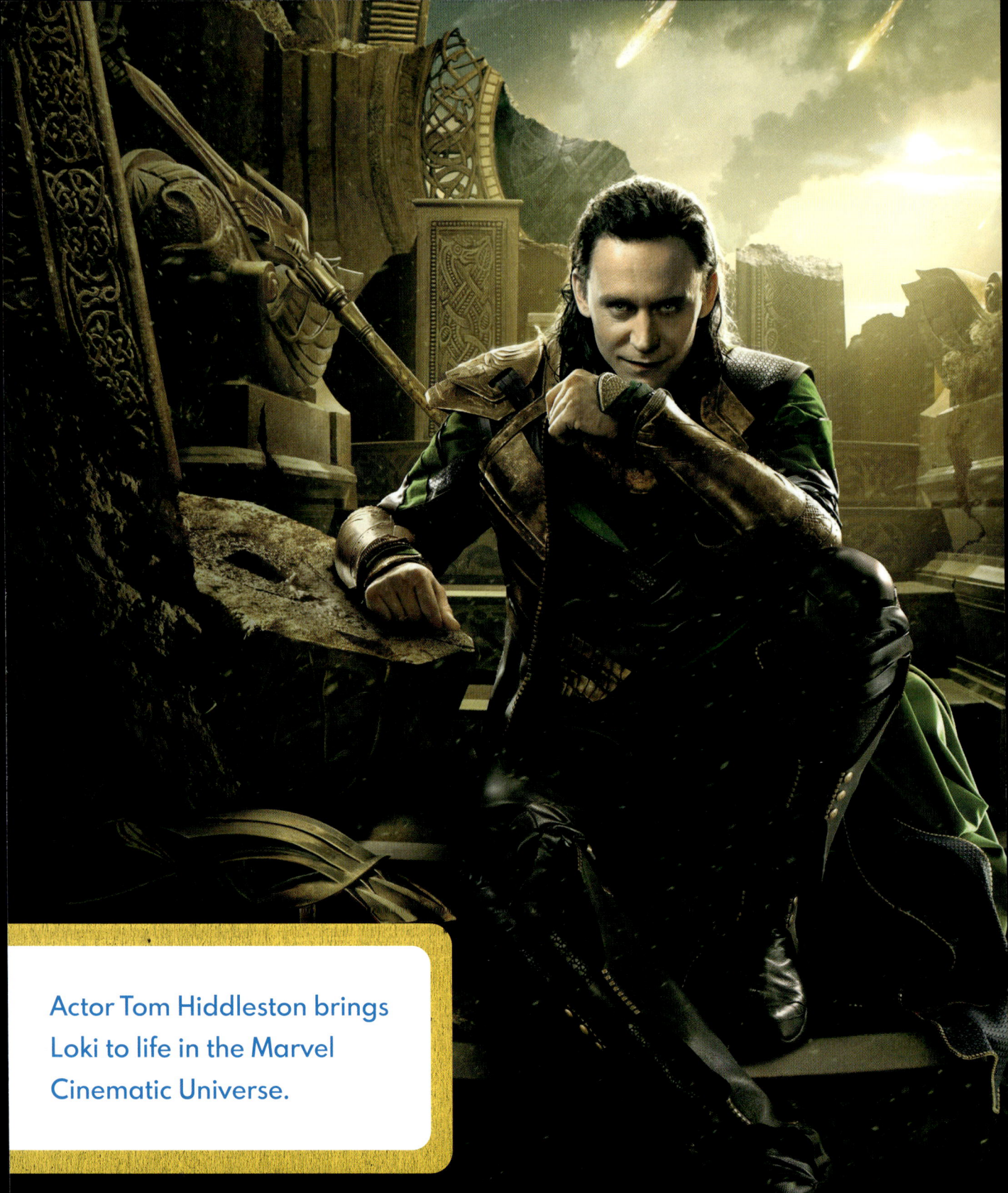

Actor Tom Hiddleston brings Loki to life in the Marvel Cinematic Universe.

CHAPTER 3

LOKI'S LEGACY

Loki is a figure who is always plotting. No one is sure what Loki will do next. This might be why he is treated differently than the other gods. The Norse people worshipped the other gods. But historians have found no evidence of worshipping Loki.

Despite this, Loki is an important figure in Norse mythology. When his pranks are harmless, the gods adore him. Loki entertains them and makes life fun. But sometimes Loki's tricks go too far. The gods punish him. Loki represents the good and bad sides all people have. He also represents change.

Loki's Punishment

Loki took his tricks too far with Baldr. Baldr was the son of Odin and Frigg. He was one of the most loved gods. Frigg had made every living thing promise not to hurt Baldr. But Frigg had not asked mistletoe to make the promise. Loki tricked the blind god Hodr into throwing mistletoe at Baldr, killing him. The gods tried to

Loki tricked Hodr into killing his brother Baldr.

bring Baldr back from the dead. But Loki foiled that plan, too.

The gods captured Loki and took him to a cave. They brought Loki's sons Vali and Narfi. Odin turned Vali into a wolf. The wolf killed Narfi. The gods tied Loki to some rocks.

The Norse people believed Loki's shaking was the cause of earthquakes.

The giantess Skadi placed a snake above the rocks. Its **venom** dripped on Loki. Sigyn stayed with Loki. She caught the venom in a bowl to save Loki's life. When the bowl got full, she had to leave to empty it. The venom would drip on Loki's face, and he would shake in pain.

Ragnarok is the end of the world. Stories say Earth will shake so hard that all chains break. Loki will be freed. He will bring a ship full of giants to fight the gods. Fenrir and

Jormungandr will join the fight. Stories say most of the gods will die in this fierce battle. Heimdall is the protector of the gods. He and Loki will die fighting each other at Ragnarok.

Loki in Art and Today

Some art created by the Norse people still exists. But there are few examples of Loki. Loki could be a horse, a fly, an old woman, or anything else. This made it hard to show what he looked like. Historians believe the Snaptun Stone from Denmark may show Loki. The face's lips are stitched together. This could show Loki after the dwarf Brokk sewed his lips together.

Loki is a god full of tricks. People often think of him as a villain. But he could also be heroic.

The Snaptun Stone is one of the few examples of Loki shown in Old Norse art.

He has been reinvented in the Marvel comics and movies. The character has some new powers. But he is still true to Loki's roots. He remains a **mischief**-maker and shape-shifter.

The Snaptun Stone

The Snaptun Stone was found on a beach in Denmark. Historians believe it was carved around 1000 BCE. It was a decorative part of a tool used in an ancient **forge**. Today it is on display at the Moesgaard Museum in Denmark.

PRIMARY SOURCE

One of the few places that describes Loki is *The Prose Edda.* Snorri Sturluson wrote this book in the 1200s. He said:

> Loki is pleasing, even beautiful to look at, but his nature is evil, and he is undependable.

Source: Snorri Sturluson. *The Prose Edda.* Translated by Jesse Byock, Penguin Classics, 2005, p. 39.

Comparing Texts

Think about the quote. Does it support the information in this chapter? Or does it give a different perspective? Explain how in a few sentences.

LEGENDARY FACTS

Loki was the Norse trickster god.

Loki had three children with the giantess Angrboda. He also had two human children with his wife Sigyn, and he was the mother of Sleipnir the horse.

Loki tricked the blind god Hodr into hurting Baldr with mistletoe. It was the only thing that could harm Baldr.

The gods punished Loki for his role in Baldr's death.

Glossary

forge
a furnace used to heat metal for shaping

mare
a female horse

mischief
playfulness that may lead to trouble

prank
a joke or mischievous act

Scandinavia
the countries of Norway, Sweden, and Denmark, and sometimes Iceland and Finland

trickster
a person who plays pranks or tricks on someone else

venom
a toxic material made by animals such as snakes that can cause pain or death

Online Resources

To learn more about Loki, visit our free resource websites below.

Visit **abdocorelibrary.com** or scan this QR code for free Common Core resources for teachers and students, including vetted activities, multimedia, and booklinks, for deeper subject comprehension.

Visit **abdobooklinks.com** or scan this QR code for free additional online weblinks for further learning. These links are routinely monitored and updated to provide the most current information available.

Learn More

Alexander, Heather. *A Child's Introduction to Norse Mythology.* Black Dog & Leventhal, 2018.

Ralphs, Matt. *Norse Myths.* DK Children, 2021.

Rea, Amy C. *Fenrir.* Abdo, 2024.

Index

About the Author

Kate Conley has been writing nonfiction books for children for more than ten years. When she is not writing, Conley spends her time reading, sewing, and solving crossword puzzles. She lives in Minnesota with her husband and two children.